A VISIT TO
France

REVISED AND UPDATED

NORTH
AMERICA

FRANCE EUROPE

ASIA

AFRICA

SOUTH
AMERICA

AUSTRALIA

Rob Alcraft

Heinemann
LIBRARY

H www.heinemann.co.uk/library
Visit our website to find out more information about Heineman

To order:
☎ Phone 44 (0) 1865 888066
🖺 Send a fax to 44 (0) 1865 314091
💻 Visit the Heinemann Bookshop at www.heinemann.co.uk/librar
catalogue and order online.

First published in Great Britain by Heinemann Library, Halley Court, Jordan Hill, Oxford OX2 8EJ, part of Pearson Education. Heinemann is a registered trademark of Pearson Education Ltd.

Editorial: Sarah Shannon
Design: Joanna Hinton-Malivoire
Picture research: Mica Brancic
Production: Duncan Gilbert

Originated by Modern Age
Printed and bound in China by South China Printing Co. Ltd

ISBN 978 0 431087276 (hardback)
12 11 10 09 08
10 9 8 7 6 5 4 3 2 1

ISBN 978 0 431087412 (paperback)
12 11 10 09 08
10 9 8 7 6 5 4 3 2 1

British Library Cataloguing in Publication Data
Alcraft, Rob 1966-
A visit to France. - New ed.
1. France – Social conditions – 1995 –   – Juvenile literature
2. France – Geography – Juvenile literature
3. France – Social life and customs – 21st century – Juvenile literature
I.Title II.France
944'.084

Acknowledgements
The publishers would like to thank the following for permission to reproduce photographs: ©Bridgeman Art Library p. **28**; ©Getty Images p. **11** (The Image Bank/Michael Melford), p. **24** (The Image Bank/Yellow Dog Productions); ©J Allan Cash pp. **17, 25**; ©Masterfile p. **13** (Bruce Fleming); ©Photolibrary p. **18** (Mauritius/Raga Raga), p. **19** (Photononstop/A J Cassaigne); ©Rex Features p. **29** (Sipa Press); ©Robert Harding Picture Library p. **9**, p. **5** (Robert Francis), p. **6** (Adam Woolfitt), p. **15** (Nik Wheeler), p. **21** (K Gillham), p. **26** (Tomlinson); ©Telegraph Colour Library p. **16** (C B Knight), p. **27** (Kathy Collins); ©Trevor Clifford p. **17**; ©Trip p. **7** (D Hastilow), p. **8** (A Tovy), p. **10** (J Braund), p. **12** (A M Bazalik), p. **22** (Ask Images), p. **20** (S Grant), p. **23** (R Cracknell).

Cover photograph of the Pyramide and Palais du Louvre, Musee du Lourve, Paris, France reproduced with permission of Robert Harding (Nigel Francis).

Our thanks to Nick Lapthorn and Clare Lewis for their help in the preparation of this book.

Every effort has been made to contact copyright holders of any material reproduced in this book. Any omissions will be rectified in subsequent printings if notice is given to the publishers.

Contents

France 4

Land 6

Landmarks 8

Homes. 10

Food 12

Clothes 14

Work 16

Transport. 18

Languages. 20

School. 22

Free time 24

Celebrations 26

The Arts. 28

Factfile 30

Glossary 31

Index. 32

Any words appearing in bold, **like this**, are explained in the Glossary.

France

France is a big country. It is in Europe.

A quarter of France is forest. There are lakes and rivers. There are gentle valleys where grapes grow. A place where grapes are grown is called a vineyard.

France is famous for its vineyards.

DOMAINE R COULY

Land

In the north of France there are green fields and **meadows**. The weather is cool, and it often rains. Farmers grow **wheat** and keep cows.

In the south of France there are high mountains, and the Mediterranean Sea. Up in the mountains it is cool and wet. By the sea it is sunny and dry.

The view from the mountainside can be very beautiful.

Landmarks

This is the Eiffel Tower. It is in the middle of Paris. Paris is the **capital** city of France. It is the biggest city in France.

The Pont du Gard bridge is 2,000 years old.

This is a bridge, called the Pont du Gard. It was built to carry water to an ancient city.

Homes

In cities like Paris most people live in flats.
Some windows have wooden **shutters**
to keep the rooms cool in summer.

Many smaller towns and villages in France are very old. There are shady squares and narrow streets. The old houses are built from stone.

The houses in villages were often built close together.

Food

Each **region** of France makes its own kinds of cheese, sausage and wine. A good snack is local cheese, with a long stick of French bread.

In France, people often have meals outside.

In France families often sit together to eat. This family is enjoying lunch outside in the garden.

Clothes

Many French people wear jeans, training shoes and colourful T-shirts, or jumpers and coats. Some people wear a special French hat called a béret.

14

Different parts of France have different costumes.

For festivals and parties people still dress up in old French costumes. Women wear white blouses, **bonnets**, and long black skirts with colourful patterns.

Work

France is famous for its **fashion**.
Some people have jobs in the fashion
industry, making and selling clothes.

Olive trees grow in the south of France.

In the country, many farmers grow olive trees. The olives can be eaten or made into oil for cooking.

Transport

France has very fast **motorways**. You have to pay to use them. One of the busiest motorways runs around Paris. This one runs over a huge bridge.

This is called a TGV train. It can go at over 300 miles per hour.

French trains are comfortable and very fast. The **canals** and rivers are busy with **barges** and boats. There are airports in most cities too.

Languages

In France people speak French. French sounds very different from English, but it uses the same alphabet.

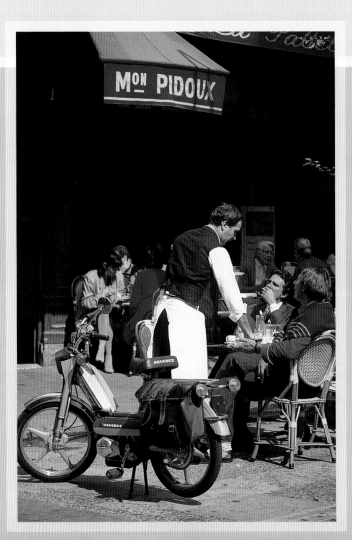

Markets are good places to hear the local french dialect.

Different **regions** of France have their own **dialects**. French is also spoken in many parts of the world.

School

Most French children go to school six days a week. Wednesday afternoons are free. French children study many subjects, including maths, geography, and English.

The mountains in France are good for skiing.

Some French schools have special holidays. The whole class will go off for a week for lessons by the beach. In the winter the class might go off to learn how to ski.

Free time

Young people play sports like football in parks or in the street. Sometimes they watch TV or visit friends. In the summer they might go swimming at the beach.

On warm summer evenings many French people like to sit in pavement cafés, and watch the world go by. Some people play a game called **pétanque**.

Pétanque is played outside in the market squares.

Celebrations

One of the biggest celebrations in France is called Mardi Gras. Everyone has a big party, and there are fireworks and **parades** along city streets.

Sometimes people dress up in old costumes for festivals.

Many French towns and villages have their own special celebration or festival. It might be on a Saint's Day, or to celebrate the **harvest**. Some are in honour of the local cheese, or that year's new wine.

The Arts

There have been many famous French painters. This is a painting by Renoir. He wanted his paintings to show how beautiful and colourful the world is.

Famous film stars
come to Cannes
for the film festival.

Making films is important in France.
In May there is a special film festival at a
town called Cannes. People come from
all over the world to see the new films.

Factfile

Name	The French Republic
Capital	France's **capital** city is called Paris.
Language	French
Population	There are 64 million people living in France.
Money	French money is called the euro.
Religions	Most French people are Christians.
Products	France makes cars, cloth, aircraft, machines and **electrical goods**. **Tourism** is also very important.

Words you can learn

bonjour (bon-jewer)	hello
au revoir (oh-rev-wa)	goodbye
oui (we)	yes
non (noh)	no
merci (ma-r-see)	thank you
S'il vous plaît (cil voo play)	please
un (urn)	one
deux (de)	two
trois (twa)	three

Glossary

barge a boat with a flat bottom. It can float in shallow water.

bonnet a kind of hat that women wear

canal a river dug by people

capital the city where the government is based

dialect the language spoken by people in one area

electrical goods things like televisions and videos which use electricity

fashion the way clothes look and what colour they are

harvest the time when fruit, vegetables and other crops are ready for the farmer to pick

meadow grassy land

motorway a big, fast road. Often they have three lanes of cars going each way.

parade special carnival in the street

pétanque a game like bowls

region a part of a country

shutters wooden flaps on each side of a window. They can be closed to keep the light out.

tourism everything to do with visiting a place on holiday

wheat plant used to make flour

Index

Eiffel Tower 8

farmers 6, 17

families 13

films 29

food 12, 13

forest 5

grapes 5

holidays 23

Mardi Gras 26

Paris 8, 10, 17

roads 18

school 22, 23